Once

POEMS

Meghan O'Rourke

W. W. Norton & Company | New York · London

For information about permission to reproduce selections from this book,
write to Permissions, W. W. Norton & Company, Inc.,
500 Fifth Avenue, New York, NY 10110

For information about special discounts for bulk purchases, please contact
W. W. Norton Special Sales at specialsales@wwnorton.com or 800-233-4830

Manufacturing by Courier Westford
Book design by Chris Welch Design
Production manager: Julia Druskin

Library of Congress Cataloging-in-Publication Data

O'Rourke, Meghan.
Once : poems / Meghan O'Rourke. — 1st ed.
    p. cm.
ISBN 978-0-393-08062-9 (hardcover)
I. Title.
PS3615.R586O53 2011
811'.6—dc23

                              2011029033

W. W. Norton & Company, Inc.
500 Fifth Avenue, New York, N.Y. 10110
www.wwnorton.com

W. W. Norton & Company Ltd.
Castle House, 75/76 Wells Street, London W1T 3QT

1 2 3 4 5 6 7 8 9 0

CONTENTS

III

ACKNOWLEDGMENTS

Grateful acknowledgment is made to the editors of the following journals, in which some of these poems appeared: *A Public Space* ("Frontier"); *Daedalus* ("Ophelia to the Court"); *Guernica* ("Chemotherapy"); *The Kenyon Review* ("Once," "Preparation," "Twenty-first Century Fireworks," "Appeal to the Self," "Anesthesia," and "My Life as a Ruler"); *The New Yorker* ("My Aunts" and "Apartment Living"); *Poetry* ("My Life as a Subject" and "On Marriage"); *Washington Square* ("Localized" and "Magnolia"); *32 Poems* ("The Resistance to Metaphor"); *The Chronicle of Higher Education* ("In Defense of Pain"); *Brooklyn Magazine* ("Mothered" and "My Mother"); *Tin House* ("Churchyard," "Sex, Again," and "Faith").

The generous support of the MacDowell Colony and the Lannan Foundation made it possible to write many of these poems. My deep gratitude is extended to those who read early drafts of this book.

I

Once

A girl ate ices
in the red summer. Bees
buzzed among the hydrangea,

heavy as plums.
Summer widened
its lens.

You would not believe
how happy she was;
her mother pulled her

through the pool till her hair
went soft. Below,
cracks spread in the vinyl

where her mother's long legs
scissored; above, wet faces
in the sun smiled.

At dusk, lamps were lit,
Vs of geese swept past,
fresh sheets shivered

on the laundry line,
and as the nights grew crisp
our souls unfolded.

Then winter arrived.
The parents bent over the daughter
tucked in her bed;

creaking from the cold,
the black walnut's roots
swelled beneath the snow.

When spring came, the home
had tilted into the tree's
long, crooked shadow. Nothing

was the same again.

Mothered

And so I woke in the city,
a daughter with two warm arms
and two folded legs.
I was given a name,
I went home to the brownstone
with four clocks,
then woke to the glow
of *The Love Boat,* a tree slicked with ice,
and a mother reading gothic novels by the TV light.
Come, tell her quick:
the shelf of snow
is loosening on the roof.
Soon it will be too warm.

My Aunts

Grew up on the Jersey Shore in the 1970s.
Always making margaritas in the kitchen,
always laughing and doing their hair up pretty,
sharing lipstick and shoes and new juice diets;
always splitting the bill to the last penny,
stealing each other's clothes,
loving one another then turning and complaining
as they walked out the door. Each one with her doe eyes,
each one younger than the last,
each older the next year, one year
further from their girlhoods of swimming
at Sandy Hook, doing jackknives off the diving board
after school, all of them
being loved by one boy and then another,
all driving farther from St. Mary's fair, farther from Atlantic City.
They used to smoke in their cars,
rolling the windows down and letting their red fingernails
hang out, little stop lights:
Stop now, before the green
comes to cover your long brown bodies.

Diagnosis

It happened so quickly
we might have gone on
discussing whether
it really existed.
But it insisted—
not a metaphor at all,
that disease.

Chemotherapy

The decomposing squirrel in the yard,
a plump sack. That night
I bled for hours, like a dumb animal.
The evening news: Mother's doing fine today.
By Wednesday, I could smell the body from the porch.
I couldn't make myself not look.
First the flies on its brown eyes,
then the mice in its tapering ribs.
Soon it looked like the remains of a fish,
a furry scalp, a plush dead thing.
I drank lemonade and gin in the shade
as the neighbor's cat stalked the bossy blue jays.
(Mothers, in this case.)
They kept up the noise for hours.
Last night it was just a skeleton,
light enough to be lifted by the wind.

Twenty-first Century Fireworks

It is a green landscape, houses stalwart
as circus ponies, American houses, wet
kids moving through them in Spandex bathing suits;
inside, sandwiches with crusts cut off,
windows flung open and striped awnings rolled out;
family portraits on the walls and generic
medicines in the cabinet: the middle classes.

It is a little beach, rocky and ugly, but
it points out into the sapphire-blue water.
The seaweed doesn't bother the children here.
This is their childhood.
Nothing hangs at the back of their minds
like a sticky pinecone, a black branch in winter snow.
Instead, there are hot dogs and parties.

It is a rambunctious barbeque,
and the uncles do flips on the trampoline,
dancing too close to the others' wives,
as if they could stop the sun from going down.
Elsewhere, the president rests on a porch with iced tea
daydreaming of the blue sea of Bermuda,
watching his gardener prune the hydrangea.

The future hasn't arrived. It is all still
a dream, a night sweat to be swum off
in a wonderland of sand and bread.
When we woke afterward, the houses
were still standing, the green just as green,
but the seaweed had thickened and the lamp
at the end of the dock had cracked.

The Great Escape

(Lake George, New York)

We came upon
the pirate's treasure
in the cool lagoon—
a plastic spill
of coins against

the painted blue;
the water splashing
 into our little boat
—chlorified—
burned

my reddened eyes.
But it looked
like sky—
and the coins
in the chest did shine:

flecks of mica,
bits of zinc and chalk.
This is where our children came,
I think, when
they wanted to invent us—

minerals mixed with clay,
growing heavier, less like air,
every day—
painted, new, hoping
to stay true.

Anticipatory Grief

It surfaces
out of tacit gray waters—
an iceberg

on which we travel
through
the unbedded

polar day,
ice tickling
a fish

as it darts
by, a seal
climbing out

of the sea. Here
is the ice
in the morning:

green, pink,
dusky-blue.
Wettening.

Then day
slides into the plot
of night.

Its colors
go cold
to the eye.

Stupid
with knowledge,
you blink

and blink.
Now black;
now pink.

When It Went to Her Brain

When I arrived, you were holding
your pants up with a tape measure—
lassoing your hips
in ever diminishing measurement.
You lie on the sectional,
staring at the TV
and fingering the fabric
as if to grasp the actual.
I ask what you want to do.
You go quiet then say
I don't know—
Mother, you don't always know my name.
On TV a hurricane beats a boat.
Gazing at the air,
you ask me, "Is that *our* wind I hear?"

Extraneous

The wind is alive, it lifts and swings;
the river is alive, it drifts past
the sugar factory;
the grass is alive, it trembles or shakes,
the ants are alive, they move through the brown grass;
the dirt is alive, moist with rain.
In endeavor and industry
the stones within the earth all live.
What then are you, captive
of glass, moving so slowly and dully?
A delinquent; nobody's darling,
a daughter in the way of the wind—

Hart

The light of the heart is blue. It is a blue chamber,
it never ends, a summer night
stretched into dawn through which a deer bounds,

ghostly, calm, turning to regard you
as you stand on the road. And then
departs, having been held only lightly by the eye.

Everything natural to us must be felt
freely, like the clambering of a vine
through the asphalt toward the sky.

The light of the heart is blue. It is a blue chamber,
with a painted wall; in its distance a deer bounds
through forest patched by sun.

Preparation

1.

I walk though the house, turning off the lights.
The lamps in the living room, where my mother and father read;
the lamp in the dining room, by the table where they eat,
the kitchen light, by the wheezing yellow Kelvinator,
the pantry light, the last lighthouse in the dark,
moths capsizing against it. . . . The farmhouse creaks,
and summer storms flicker at the horizon—
electricity over the trees, an EKG.
In the field, the horses sleep on their feet.
What is the grass to them?
What makes them startle as we approach in the morning,
bearing fallen apples?

2.

When I was a girl we went every summer
to a house on a dirt road by a thawing mountain river
and a culvert where the water roared.
My brother and I waded all day in the stream,
shoving the dog away,
pulling up rocks and building a dam,
until we could dunk ourselves

in the pooled cold.
We wanted to see if we could
change the river, stop it
from pressing through the culvert
down into the shadowy pine forest.

3.

Sick mother, greener world.
The white manes of the clouds, the chlorine of the pool,
fewer words, more to be described.
The horses, the field, the house,
the Adirondack chairs where she and I slept one afternoon,
the pool, the sun that burned our skin, the laundry
my father hadn't done for a month,
the couch on which she slept all day, then
the other couch on which she slept all day,
the umbilical IV, the bathroom
where she got sick, the hall where he listened.
I sat in the grass, the dogs
licking my toes, ants crawling over me.
The blue light hurt my eyes.
A shirt came flapping off the laundry line
like a sail ~~or a shroud~~ —no, like a sail.

4.

I climb on a black-sailed boat
and set out into the lake
beside the drafty farmhouse.
In the middle of the lake stands an island;
on the island, a hospital bed,
and a woman laboring to breathe.
In the wind the reeds shiver.
Sometimes she moans
and I step forward
to press the morphine pump,
and she twitches and sighs.

When I wake, I stand
in the bedroom window,
closing the blinds, opening them,
lamp blinking into the dark.
I can see the island from here.

5.

But you have seen nothing.
You turn the lights on and off
and listen to your mother breathe,
asleep beside the Christmas tree,
her hands curled to her face.
A week ago she climbed the stairs
to bed, one step at a time,
pausing on the landing,
offering up her cheek and that old "good night":
"I love you to death."
You cannot prepare.
In the morning, pasteboard snow,
a masquerade dawn,
the horses swaying toward the fence
and nosing the ground for apples
frozen in the snowdrifts.

Elegy: Hill Without Scar

Christmas Day

That winter day was the last you remembered.
The shutters of the house were open.
The snow lay on the ground like cold and cracking embers.
Inside a fire, an evergreen, a slender iris by the bed.
The sky and the moon were a gateway and a token.
Your last day is the first I remember.
Each morning is a token and an ember, a fly-bitten flinch.
The dog comes wreathing through the door.
Fire haggles in the chimney, the black feet creep.
The bed is empty and the bed is heavy.
The moon is a gate or a token, who can be sure.
Tokens go under the tongues of the dead.
The dead are the first to be embers.
They do not remember the thawing ice, or wine and spice.
You sleep like an ember, a token, a door.

II

Frontier

I wandered to what I thought
was the empire's frontier,
a river of sand, a strip of paper mills.
I met with the tinkers and the tailors
hawking their wares,
I passed under the three bridges
where the fires were,
and sang *Tweedle-hee, tweedle-ha,*
a penny for a saw.
I paid a toll to the taker
then sold my blood
for money. I needed to eat:
plastic-wrapped chicken, cookies
and chocolate. At times,
I felt sick, intoxicated
by BPA and mercury.
At other times I fasted and the stars
stumbled clear from the vault.
Up there, the universe stands around drunk.
I hope the Lord is kind to us,
for we engrave our every mistake,
teasing and repenting,
coming clean for his sake.

Appeal to the Self

Have the dowagers of delusion visited you again
in their fat pink shoes,
creeping softly over the Persian rugs
of your creaking, boarded mind?
It's time to get up and air the room.
Once you were an explorer, now you are Elizabeth Barrett,
only stupider and more prone to TV-watching.
Outside, cell phones buzz like digital cicadas,
and the air green, green. But you have come up here
to rave inside the tower you call a brain.
You might as well be daubed
in mud and growing feathers. No one will ever notice
the difference between what you say and what you mean.
What you lost is what everybody else lost,
the boy who first screwed you on a rug some way
you can't quite remember. Who are you to mourn it?
There's the rub: the plain old human emotions
have become "clichéd."
But they still exist. That boy
is an actor now, proclaiming grief for art and money.
The losses are yours for good.
So come sing with me and be my love,
there is no one else but you, the voices in my head.

My Life as a Subject

I.

Because I was born in a kingdom,
there was a king. At times
the king was a despot; at other times,
not. Axes flashed in the road

at night, but if you closed your eyes
sitting on the well-edge
amongst your kinspeople
and sang the ballads
then the silver did not appear
to be broken.

Such were the circumstances.
They made a liar out of me.
Did they change my spirit?
Kith in the night.
The cry of owls. A bird fight.

II.

We also had a queen,
whetted by the moon. And
we her subjects,
softening in her sight.

III.

What one had
the others had to
have too. Soon
parrots bloomed
in all the city gardens, and
every daughter
had a jeweled tuning fork.

IV.

Learning to hunt in the new empire,
the king invited his subjects
to send him their knives.
He tested these knives on oranges,
pomegranates, acorn squash,
soft birches, stillborns, prisoners
who had broken rules. He used
them on the teeth of traitors.

V.

When strangers massed at the border,
the courtiers practiced
subjection of the foreign. The court
held a procession
of twine, rope,
gold, knives, and
prostitutes with their vials of white
powder. Smoke coursed into the courtyard,

and we wrought hunger upon
the bodies of strangers. I am sure you
can imagine
it, really what need
is there for me to tell you.
You were a stranger once too, and I
brought rope.

VI.

Afterward,
I slept, and let
the dealers
come to me alone
with their ointments and
their powders.

VII.

At night, we debated
the skin of language,
questioned what might
be revealed inside:
a soft pink fruit,

a woman in a field.
Or a shadow, sticky and loose
as old jam. Our own
dialect was abstract,
we wished to understand
not how things were
but what spectacle we might
make from them.

VIII.

One day a merchant came to court
and brought moving pictures,
the emperor's new delight.
He tacked dark cloth
to the windows and turned off
the lights, cranking the machine and the film
like a needle and thread,
making stories we could
insinuate our cold bodies
into and find warmth. Light;
dark. And the sliding images of courtiers
merrily balancing monkeys
on their heads, as if this
were an adequate story.

IX.

And our queen, that hidden
self. What became
of her? Slid into the night
like a statue, shivered
into shadows. Knowing as a spider
in retreat. The web
her mind, and in it, the fly.

X.

On Sundays, we flew kites
to ensure our joy
was seen by those who
threatened
to threaten us. The thread
spooling out high
in the purple sky
and silver-gelatin films being made,
sliding through the cranking machine
so that the barbarians could know
we made images of ourselves
coated in precious metal

and sent them away
indifferent to our wealth.

I miss the citrus
smell of spring
on the plaza filled
with young
and long-limbed kite flyers.

XI.

Do I have anything
to add? Only that
I obeyed my king, my
kind, I was not faithless.
Should I be punished
for that? It is true
the pictures slipping
through the spindle
cause me pain. I know
the powdered drugs
we coated our fingers
with made us thirsty
and sometimes cruel.

But I was born
with a spirit, like you.
I have woken, you see,
and I wish to be
made new.

On Marriage

Stone by stone, body by body in the grass:
for this we trade our lone compass,

become swans instead, adrift in glaze-
light, kilned in the arms of each other

into vessel-vassal new. Or shrew,
as the case may be. What would you do?

Listen to the footsteps in the thistles.
Put the kettle on for tea, and whisper it to me.

Mala Mala

Strangler figs twine up the leadwood tree
outside the window of the hut—
at noon, the bushveld swells with heat
and the animals sleep.
In three days the rain
has crowned the brown land
green, obscuring
the hill across the river.
Amidst its cloaking growth
the pregnant leopard stalks
an impala, paws slipping
through the prickly grass. . . .
A plane loops lazily overhead.
Over the sands its shadow spreads.
Like your stain on my body
after all is said and done—

~~no, like the stain on any body~~
~~when all is said and done~~

Churchyard

Who will remember us
when the light breaks
over the western valley

and the trash stirs,
the flood having come
with its red waters

and washed
our graves away?
I was a person

once, I believe.
I lived in a house
with lights in the windows.

As I walked down the street,
I felt ecstatic: my soul stood outside
the horizons of the known.

But commerce kept
drawing it in
and over time it grew

fainter, less visible,
smudged by the vast
declarations of a nation

that loved it
and wanted it, just had
to have it.

In the Same Boat

The pilot is sleep-steering.
He thinks he's flying a plane;
the northern lights beckon.
The river seems bigger than ever.

I wander down the deck
in search of an official.
Every time I spot a man in gold and red
he turns away from me.

Children blow balloons by the prow.
Mother Goose is playing Spite & Malice
with the Minister of Defense.
In the pool, a military cadet washes her hair.

I sit down with an old demon
and a tarot pack. Needless
to say, he turns up death.
The boat charges on

toward the devil's gap.
All the leaders of the cruise,
I see, have been dreaming
the same dream,

a night where palaces
flame white against a black sky,
and our arctic hearts melt at the valor
of their empirical imagination.

Theory vs. Practice

Our ménage à trois by candlelight—;
the various absurdities: black lace,
pink mules, a little-bo-peep teddy.

Afterward, bad Champagne
in the kitchen of the pied-à-terre.
The mind is an unforgettable red space.

But I, I can't escape this place;—
the steep of ridged limbs,
the mountainous dark pining;

and love, the flickering hood of flame.

Ophelia to the Court

My shoes are unpolished, my words smudged.
I come to you undressed (the lord, he whispers
smut; that man, he whispers such). I bend
my thoughts, I submit, but a bird
keeps flying from my mind, it slippers
my feet and sings—barren world,
I have been a little minx in it, not at all
domestic, not at all clean, not at all blinking
at my lies. First he thought he had a wife, then
(of course) he thought he had a whore. All
I wanted (if I may speak for myself) was: more.
If only one of you had said, I hold
your craven breaking soul, I see the pieces,
I feel them in my hands, idle silver, idle gold.
You see I cannot speak without telling what I am.
I disobey the death you gave me, love.
If you must be, then be not with me.

Anesthesia

Say I was searching for God.
I was in a hospital with an IV in my arm,
brittle plastic stem. I put my hand in my mouth
and the nurses took it out.
When I woke they said I'd been speaking for hours.
The machines blinked silver around me.
What took place while I was asleep?
Where had I been that I couldn't remember?
The childhood farmhouse, full of light?

But no cotton drifted through the sun.
No grass turned dun in the shadows.
No cars drove on the road just out of sight
but within earshot. You forgot
who you were. People came to your bed
and told you they loved you.
How could you know? You didn't remember
the past, you just felt it slipping out of your grasp,
like wheat in the chute of the silo
before you were born to think *me, me, me.*

Love Poem

Coyotes on the mesa,
talking to the moon.
The frozen scatter of stars.
Antelope grazing in the dried-up creek.
The hardened sleep
of buttes upon the plain.
Sorrow for everything
done, undone again.

Apartment Living

So those despotic loves have become known to you,
rubbing cold hands up your thighs,
leaving oily trails,
whispering, *Just how you like it, right?*
Upstairs the sorority girls are playing charades
again, smoking cigarettes, wearing shifts, burning
pain into their synapses.
Life is a needle. And now it pricks you:
your attempts at decadence
tire the earth and tire you. The etymology
of "flag" as in "to signal to stop"
is unknown. It is time to sit and watch. Don't
call that one again, he's pitiless in his self-certainty.
You used to be so.
You laid your black dress on the bed.
You stepped in your heels over sidewalk cracks.
You licked mint and sugar from the cocktail mixer,
singing nonsense songs,
and the strangers, they sang along.

My Life as a Ruler

I.

The world, when I met it,
lay about in broken pieces—
a neglected toy. A red hill
here; a river valley there,
green and languid; a bridge
rusting over an oil-slicked lake.
To the west and south, the tribes
had warred until their cities smoked
and their children faded, wraithed
by whooping cough.

All I did was pick up the pieces.
I caused them to be put together
like the parts of a chair.

II.

When I was young, I often
saw my parents
naked. What a delicate
business they were.
And what was I?
Neither the doctor nor the nurse.
I was the knife;
I caused the injury.

III.

When fall begins to glitter
in the green leaves,
I grow anxious.
The barbarians will
ride out. They love the goldenness
of death, how it grieves
the eye to see such richness
as the river ebbs
and the trees unfleur—

To Nineveh I write:
Bring me forty bushels of wheat,
and forty of rice,
each bushel weighing more than one donkey
can carry, within the fortnight—.
If you do not do this,
you will surely die.
And then I wait.

IV.

When I came to the throne,
I gave children birds
in their throats. We took
knives and made cuts
where the voice should be,
each cord becoming a song.
Now in the schools we have
red-wing cardinals, bluebirds,
thrashers, yellow-speckled hens,
parakeets, even, now and then,
the nightingale.

V.

I grow hungry
to be a knife again.

VI.

My subject, you
think you have a choice, but
you don't: you are me,
and I love you as only
a ruler can love—
unmercifully.
Do not be sentimental
about mercy. It leaves
so much up to choice.

VII.

That year was a beautiful lie,
the year my love lived with me
and we spent the summer
wading into the Nile
as the floods receded,
letting the current carry our bodies
around the bend—.

The water so strong
you had to dive in
before it knocked
you off your feet
and pulled you
under—
          he showed me how to pick thistle
for tea. We came upon
a leopard in the grass
and she hissed at us.
One day he hissed at me,
slapping away my hands,
asking "What kind of person
does THAT?"

No one loves the person
who holds power
over his survival.

VIII.

I was sad, and I
stuffed your throats
with birds.

IX.

I cut the sea
with a knife
because the sea
would not stop for me.
And still it broke:
not under me,
but over me.

X.

Of course I hate my power.
Bored, I ply lithe men with faience,
require the dancing girls to moan and plaint.
I lick kohl from their salty eyelids.
I take the gold from the braziers and burn strangers' flesh.
None of it satisfies me.
I thought the world's trouble
lay in its shards. So I resolved to hold
the shards to my heart.
Now I find the trouble is the night,
which keeps coming, though
I command it not to.

XI.

Tonight I wash my hands and sing
old songs. I call my friend,
I love to watch him dance.
He drinks wine impetuously.
He will leave my care
when another's light kiss
vaccinates him against my illness,

some sweet-tempered almondine thing
lighting firecrackers between her feet
in the summer grass—not one
like me, nearly frozen up with cruelty—

XII.

And so I go to work.
My nation is the grass,
these broken bridges,
men and women burning
beside the crumbling churches.
I keep them alive with my words.
I am vigilant.
I am the grass and the birds
and I eat them too.

III

Magnolia

Come in out of the storm.
The glass on the windows is going black.
Outside, the neighbor's tree
has begun to bud, deceived
by the unruly warmth.
How much silence there was
until the snow began to fall,
soft, soft, soft, and strewn
upon frozen fresh-bloomed flowers.
They creaked and cried,
wild colts being broken.

Sonogram

In her frame I curl
in question, gray dot
amidst a white field,
polar night
in which I drift, chilled,
akimbo,
blanketed. She creaks;
this sky is ice.
I thaw, licking
my way into life, tongue warm,
eyes focusing. . . .
How soon
the sun comes!
And with it, of course,
the blank night.

After Her Death

I lived in an underworld.

Snowflakes on my eyes, fingers curled,
I made the bed my home,
curtaining my eyes from the sun—
in my sleep she and I
                          passed each other
side to side, and did not touch.
And my hands, O, my hands
cracked,
        my knuckles bled,
shade to shade I bent
leaning down into your ground—

(One night at midnight I got a glimpse
of the oiled wing
of the thing that courses

—spendthrift—

through the iron-cored
underworld; but it is not
mine to name—.)

I tell you this to say:
I believe, Mother, in the things you see.
I look where you look.
I will not let you rescind
like this winterwind.
I have burned the blindfold
            but kept the hood—

it will protect me from your ice.

Sex, Again

It's like a movie—the machine whirs,
feeling whispers to itself in a dark room,
a desert of pain and suspense.
Torn tickets litter the floor.

Two bodies in a corner
try to rewind the distance between us.
Finger, tongue, mirage, a sailboat,
the unexamined sun.

Queer with suspense, you fast-forward the reel,
brushing the dust and licking
at the scratches, a hermit operator,
picturing freedom in each frame.

The madrigal moon silvers the night.
You have small hands and a ring.
To what am I permitted to submit?
Red light, slip me through the sand.

Inventory

(after the Texas Revised Inventory of Grief)

    I.

I opened my mother's jewelry box:
pins and rings and tangled necklaces,
a Sloan-Kettering appointment card,
Puck the cocker spaniel's Purina ID,
the one I wore on a string around my neck
for a year after his death;
a pair of plastic skeleton earrings,
a dull gold medal, a folded blue ribbon,
a pencil drawing: house, flowers, the sun and a cat,
graphite-smudged, smiling.

A mess of a box, a private crypt—
I dump it on my bed
onto a sheet like the one
she lay under
when they carried her out the living room door,
a sheet of clean sky.

    2.

Stay another night,
she says while making pie,

apples softening
in her hands,
peels dropping to the floor.
—"Stay": as if I
could insert
my small self
between her
and the grave,
push back the blank with my fist.
I wake curled
in a wish.

3.

The first thirty-eight days
after her death:

a violin bow
poised over your cracked-open chest,
playing on your heart,
the well-rosined strings creaking
      back and forth
      back and forth

4.

On a roan horse ridden at a canter
past power plants and rose gardens,
along fogged roads and cold knolls,
across the thistle field and past the idle pulleys—
      she laughed as she rode.

After two years and seven months she died.
We found the horse on the side of the road.
We took her off its back and burned her
body, her warm black eyes—
with the ashes we made a sign
      in the soot-thick air:
      Horseman, pass by.

5.

Lilacs, lemon, and chamomile
my mother loved as much as I—

6.

A mother makes a daughter
        by dividing.
The hands, the nose, the feet
all grow by multiplying,
delicate and brazen.

It does not escape you
that the tumors in the lungs and liver, too,
        grow by multiplying,
indiscriminate, lacking ears
and mouths and eyes to see
what they do:

        Selfish daughters,
        greedy thieves
growing
        just for the sake of growth—;

7.

All spring the rain
would not end

and the mud grew unruly,
staining the shoes
worn grimly all spring
when the rain would not end.
  O, it *did* end—
the damp wet earth
that got on your legs
whenever you went for a run
  eventually dried.
The rain would not end,
but the mud came off in the bath.

  8.

The hand-tooled belt
a man used
as a whip
across your back
to make a ship
on which you both might climb
to be carried
into a different clime—
that ship unsound,

that whip a belt
around your waist,
whistling *waste, waste*. . . .
—And then, sharply: Taste.

    9.

The lemon ammonia
of your newly clean home
makes you think of nothing
but the very end,
        the body letting go
its waste,
the whisper-soft breath
        giving up the ghost.

    10.

Once when you were young
you climbed a tree you could not
        climb down from.

A neighbor thought
    you were a monkey
and brought out his gun.
        Perversely, you closed your eyes.

Then your mother found
you and gathered you in her arms.
        The softness was soft.
        Her hair was clean.
She meant everything.

You laid your head against her shoulder
and played with the tiger's eye earring
        stranded high
        in her strung black hair,
a muddied, waxen star—

In Defense of Pain

So now the sleighs have slid away
and the ice on the trees cracks,
sharp champagne pops, toasts
silenced by the snow-bound woods.
Half asleep beneath an eiderdown
stitched with dawn-red thread,
you are in a painting, walking the high slopes
of a mountain above the timberline.
Even as you climb you are striding past the overlook.
Below, the forest shudders in wind.
You have been here before,
in this painting, on this gray-green rock,
staring across the valley—
for years, you thought there was a door
on the other side, a sky scrap,
redbirds and red cedars and more.
Now you see the door
is the scar of a bulldozed home:
the red earth ugly
on the mountainside, a scalp
bleeding from a sore.
Does that mean you won't
come here anymore?

My Mother

Grew up the oldest of six in the nineteen sixties.
Left home at seventeen in the company of a reprobate,
my father, twenty-three, whose wavy hair
was soon to grow long. Channeling his inner Irish aristocrat,
he called himself the Prince of Breiffni.
Irish too, black-eyed, she wore bell-bottoms
and halter-tops, knee-high boots and a faux-leopard-spotted coat;
she liked to bake, to smoke pot, to read Gogol,
was quiet until she was not, rolling her eyes at
a pun, a pretension, always happy to see her friends;
wearing brown saddle shoes and a merit pin on her chest
until the day she was kicked out of school.
Favorite color, blue. Preferred practice to theory.
Even when she was weary, even after the chemo,
she liked horses and swimming, eating bread with jam,
driving too fast in her leased BMW,
making pies and quilts, always rejecting guilt, licking juice from
    her lips.
O come down from your weeping cherry,
Mother, and look at how we have scattered
your ashes only in our minds, unable
to let you leave the house—.

Localized

Underneath the white coverlet
you began to see only the dead,
until you slept in an infinite regress,
history textbooks curling on the counter,
ants marching back into the sugar bowl.
One night you sat in the bath
listening for that sole birdcall,
the sky close to your head,
blue, lacerated, clear—

Pike's Peak

In the shadow
of the mountain
quarters click

in the arcades.
Staving off
the Centipede,

children lick
their cotton candy,
sticky-pink with sun.

The pinball
machines gleam,
a tabby cat preens. . . .

By the red rock
I sit remembering
my "youth."

How we drove there
and the shadow
of an idea pursued me

and the land
turned green with envy
of all the new

things—
curios twist in the
shop windows,

digital bells
ring out
in the glade.

The Resistance to Metaphor

I wanted the world to be a fact.
The time for metaphor was over.
I got in the artist's refurbished Range Rover
and drove to where the antelope
lay curled in the desert.
I studied the horizon: buttes,
fences, prickly pears, goatherds.
Two hawks circled the dump.
The future was a duty.
Spring would soon arrive,
and with it more sky, and the firs,
the firs on the mountain would turn to fire.

Seven Months Later

I don't feel you in the air.
Maybe you grew tired of the earth, maybe
the dead do. Summer tomatoes and leaves
green with sun don't matter to the eternal—?
But I am still here,
walking among the shy midsummer trees,
drinking tea.
I go through doors and into cars,
hair wet, a mustard stain on my sleeve.
But you are like a weeping cherry—
the sun nourishes you. No; not even the sun.
Do you need anything?

At night I sleep poorly. When I dream
of your face, the papery cotton sheets
go cool as your hand used to be.
Downstairs, you are there, in the box
I will not look at.
The world is askew without you,
like a lock jimmied by a thief.
When together now, four of us, not five,
we eat quickly, nibbling the corn to the husk.
Even the dogs have gotten quiet
in your absence. The other morning,

I sat in your chair reading.
Next door the mower started up.
I startled at the noise.
Nothing should be growing.

Still

The daughter wakes to a world
encased in ice—
the pine trees stiff with it.

Her mother lies
in the living room
on a metal-barred bed,

the Christmas tree
pointing upward,
the oxygen machine wheezing.

The house is festive—
holiday greens and red ribbons
tied to the doorknobs,

white lights strung along
the porch—the dogs trip
in them and bark.

The mother opens her eyes
and looks at the daughter
reading on the couch;

once, perhaps,
she smiles—
with her high black bun

she looks like a girl
herself. All night
her daughter sleeps

beside her, wakes to her small,
low groans, and presses the bolus
to keep the morphine going,

staring at the Christmas lights,
letting them blur in her eyes.
The dogs keep close to the bed.

She can remember swimming
in her grandmother's pool.
She can see the blue water,

the ice tea mix suspended
in the yellow glass,
those afternoon hours

a painting where they might
have swum and read books
forever, a painting

where the artist had drawn
a gray leaf,
striped with red,

a leaf you might imagine
if you lived underground
and couldn't remember the sun.

Faith

And into my doubt
the bells rang—

mourning doves and,
later, voices in song.

The dim breath
that left my body, the sliding

away of love,

scattered hairs
on the white sheets—

bodies are used
like weapons

it is what
they are meant for.

But the door, the door
is in the mind. . . .

You can step out of
violence and into

sky.

"Once" is for Barbara O'Rourke.

The italicized portion of "My Life as a Ruler" is derived from a letter that was displayed in wall text at the Oriental Institute of the University of Chicago.

"Hart" is for J.S.